I0470919

The Key Facts™ on

Cyprus

Essential Information on Cyprus

By Patrick W. Nee

The Internationalist®

www.internationalist.com

<u>**The Internationalist**</u>®

International Business, Investment, and Travel

Published by:

The Internationalist Publishing Company

96 Walter Street/ Suite 200

Boston, MA 02131, USA

Tel: 617-354-7722

www.internationalist.com

PN@internationalist.com

Table Of Contents

Chapter 1: Background

Chapter 2: Geography

Chapter 3: People and Society

Chapter 4: Government and Key Leaders

Chapter 5: Economy

Chapter 6: Energy

Chapter 7: Communications

Chapter 8: Transportation

Chapter 9: Military

Chapter 10: Transnational Issues

Chapter 1: Background

A former British colony, Cyprus became independent in 1960 following years of resistance to British rule. Tensions between the Greek Cypriot majority and Turkish Cypriot minority came to a head in December 1963, when violence broke out in the capital of Nicosia. Despite the deployment of UN peacekeepers in 1964, sporadic intercommunal violence continued forcing most Turkish Cypriots into enclaves throughout the island. In 1974, a Greek Government-sponsored attempt to seize control of Cyprus was met by military intervention from Turkey, which soon controlled more than a third of the island. In 1983, the Turkish Cypriot-occupied area declared itself the "Turkish Republic of Northern Cyprus" ("TRNC"), but it is recognized only by Turkey. The election of a new Cypriot president in 2008 served as the impetus for the UN to encourage both the Greek Cypriot and Turkish Cypriot communities to reopen unification negotiations. In September 2008, the leaders of the two communities began negotiations under UN auspices aimed at reuniting the divided island. The talks are ongoing. The entire island entered the EU on 1 May 2004, although the EU acquis - the body of common rights and obligations - applies only to the areas under the internationally recognized government, and is suspended in the areas administered by

Turkish Cypriots. However, individual Turkish Cypriots able to document their eligibility for Republic of Cyprus citizenship legally enjoy the same rights accorded to other citizens of European Union states.

Chapter 2: Geography

Location:

Middle East, island in the Mediterranean Sea, south of Turkey

Geographic coordinates:

35 00 N, 33 00 E

Map references:

Europe

Area:

Total: 9,251 sq km (of which 3,355 sq km are in north Cyprus)

Country comparison to the world: 171

Land: 9,241 sq km

Water: 10 sq km

Area - comparative:

About 0.6 times the size of Connecticut

Land boundaries:

Total: 150.4 km (approximately)

Border sovereign base areas: Akrotiri 47.4 km, Dhekelia 103 km (approximately)

Coastline:

648 km

Maritime claims:

Territorial sea: 12 nm

Contiguous zone: 24 nm

Continental shelf: 200 m depth or to the depth of
exploitation

Climate:

Temperate; Mediterranean with hot, dry summers and cool
winters

Terrain:

Central plain with mountains to north and south; scattered
but significant plains along southern coast

Elevation extremes:

Lowest point: Mediterranean Sea 0 m

Highest point: Mount Olympus 1,951 m

Natural resources:

Copper, pyrites, asbestos, gypsum, timber, salt, marble,
clay earth pigment

Land use:

Arable land: 10.81%

Permanent crops: 4.32%

Other: 84.87% (2005)

Irrigated land:

460 sq km (2003)

Total renewable water resources:

0.4 cu km (2005)

Freshwater withdrawal (domestic/industrial/agricultural):

Total: 0.21 cu km/yr (27%/1%/71%)

Per capita: 250 cu m/yr (2000)

Natural hazards:

Moderate earthquake activity; droughts

Environment - current issues:

Water resource problems (no natural reservoir catchments, seasonal disparity in rainfall, sea water intrusion to island's largest aquifer, increased salination in the north); water pollution from sewage and industrial wastes; coastal degradation; loss of wildlife habitats from urbanization

Environment - international agreements:

Party to: Air Pollution, Air Pollution-Nitrogen Oxides, Air Pollution-Persistent Organic Pollutants, Air Pollution-Sulfur 94, Biodiversity, Climate Change, Climate Change-Kyoto Protocol, Desertification, Endangered Species, Environmental Modification, Hazardous Wastes, Law of the Sea, Marine Dumping, Ozone Layer Protection, Ship Pollution, Wetlands

Signed, but not ratified: none of the selected agreements

Geography - note:

The third largest island in the Mediterranean Sea (after Sicily and Sardinia)

Chapter 3: People and Society

Nationality:

Noun: Cypriot(s)

Adjective: Cypriot

Ethnic groups:

Greek 77%, Turkish 18%, other 5% (2001)

Languages:

Greek (official), Turkish (official), English

Religions:

Greek Orthodox 78%, Muslim 18%, other (includes Maronite and Armenian Apostolic) 4%

Population:

1,155,403 (July 2013 est.)

Country comparison to the world: 160

Age structure:

0-14 years: 15.9% (male 93,179/female 87,941)

15-24 years: 16.1% (male 99,784/female 83,793)

25-54 years: 46.8% (male 278,330/female 254,355)

55-64 years: 10.5% (male 56,719/female 62,286)

65 years and over: 10.7% (male 52,900/female 68,784)

(2012 est.)

Median age:

total: 35.1 years

male: 33.8 years

female: 36.9 years (2012 est.)

Population growth rate:

1.571% (2012 est.)

country comparison to the world: 76

Birth rate:

11.44 births/1,000 population (2012 est.)

country comparison to the world: 168

Death rate:

6.48 deaths/1,000 population (July 2012 est.)

country comparison to the world: 151

Net migration rate:

10.75 migrant(s)/1,000 population (2012 est.)

country comparison to the world: 11

Urbanization:

urban population: 70% of total population (2010)

rate of urbanization: 1.3% annual rate of change (2010-15 est.)

Major cities - population:

NICOSIA (capital) 240,000 (2009)

Sex ratio:

at birth: 1.05 male(s)/female

under 15 years: 1.06 male(s)/female

15-64 years: 1.09 male(s)/female

65 years and over: 0.77 male(s)/female

total population: 1.04 male(s)/female (2011 est.)

Maternal mortality rate:

10 deaths/100,000 live births (2010)

country comparison to the world: 154

Infant mortality rate:

total: 9.05 deaths/1,000 live births

country comparison to the world: 152

male: 10.72 deaths/1,000 live births

female: 7.3 deaths/1,000 live births (2012 est.)

Life expectancy at birth:

total population: 78 years

country comparison to the world: 56

male: 75.21 years

female: 80.92 years (2012 est.)

Total fertility rate:

1.46 children born/woman (2013 est.)

country comparison to the world: 195

Health expenditures:

6% of GDP (2010)

country comparison to the world: 106

Physicians density:

2.3 physicians/1,000 population (2006)

Hospital bed density:

3.8 beds/1,000 population (2008)

Sanitation facility access:

improved:

urban: 100% of population

rural: 100% of population

total: 100% of population

HIV/AIDS - adult prevalence rate:

0.1% (2003 est.)

country comparison to the world: 120

HIV/AIDS - people living with HIV/AIDS:

fewer than 1,000 (2007 est.)

country comparison to the world: 139

Obesity - adult prevalence rate:

12.3% (2003)

country comparison to the world: 48

Education expenditures:

4.1% of GDP (2007)

country comparison to the world: 99

Literacy:

definition: age 15 and over can read and write

total population: 97.6%

male: 98.9%

female: 96.3% (2001 census)

School life expectancy (primary to tertiary education):

total: 14 years

male: 14 years

female: 14 years (2008)

Unemployment, youth ages 15-24:

total: 16.6%

country comparison to the world: 72

male: 16.1%

female: 17% (2010)

Chapter 4: Government and Key Leaders

Country name:

> conventional long form: Republic of Cyprus
>
> conventional short form: Cyprus
>
> local long form: Kypriaki Dimokratia/Kibris Cumhuriyeti
>
> local short form: Kypros/Kibris
>
> note: the Turkish Cypriot community, which administers the northern part of the island, refers to itself as the "Turkish Republic of Northern Cyprus" or "TRNC" (Kuzey Kibris Turk Cumhuriyeti or KKTC)

Government type:

> republic
>
> note: a separation of the two ethnic communities inhabiting the island began following the outbreak of communal strife in 1963; this separation was further solidified after the Turkish intervention in July 1974, following a Greek military-junta-supported coup attempt that gave the Turkish Cypriots de facto control in the north; Greek Cypriots control the only internationally recognized government; on 15 November 1983 Turkish Cypriot "President" Rauf DENKTAS declared independence and the formation of a "Turkish Republic of Northern Cyprus" ("TRNC"), which is recognized only by Turkey

Capital:

name: Nicosia (Lefkosia/Lefkosa)

geographic coordinates: 35 10 N, 33 22 E

time difference: UTC+2 (7 hours ahead of Washington, DC during Standard Time)

daylight saving time: +1hr, begins last Sunday in March; ends last Sunday in October

Administrative divisions:

6 districts; Ammochostos (Famagusta; all but a small part controlled by Turkish Cyprus), Keryneia (Kyrenia; the only district completely controlled by Turkish Cyprus), Larnaka (Larnaca; a small part controlled by Turkish Cyprus), Lemesos (Limassol), Lefkosia (Nicosia; a small part controlled by Turkish Cyprus), Pafos (Paphos); note - the five districts of Turkish Cyprus are Gazimagusa (Famagusta), Girne (Kyrenia), Guzelyurt (Morphou), Lefkosia (Nicosia) and Iskele (Trikomo)

Independence:

16 August 1960 (from the UK); note - Turkish Cypriots proclaimed self-rule on 13 February 1975 and independence in 1983, but these proclamations are only recognized by Turkey

National holiday:

Independence Day, 1 October (1960); note - Turkish Cypriots celebrate 15 November (1983) as "Independence Day"

Constitution:

16 August 1960

note: from December 1963, the Turkish Cypriots no longer participated in the government; negotiations to create the basis for a new or revised constitution to govern the island and for better relations between Greek and Turkish Cypriots have been held intermittently since the mid-1960s; in 1975, following the 1974 Turkish intervention, Turkish Cypriots created their own constitution and governing bodies within the "Turkish Federated State of Cyprus," which they then called the "Turkish Republic of Northern Cyprus (TRNC)" when the Turkish Cypriots declared independence in 1983; a new constitution for the "TRNC" passed by referendum on 5 May 1985, although the "TRNC" remains unrecognized by any country other than Turkey

Legal system:

mixed legal system of English common law and civil law with Greek Orthodox religious law influence

International law organization participation:

accepts compulsory ICJ jurisdiction with reservations; accepts ICCt jurisdiction

Suffrage:

18 years of age; universal

Executive branch:

chief of state: President Nicos ANASTASIADES (since 28 February 2013); note - the president is both the chief of state and head of government; post of vice president is currently vacant; under the 1960 constitution, the post is reserved for a Turkish Cypriot

head of government: President Nicos ANASTASIADES (since 28 February 2013)

cabinet: Council of Ministers appointed jointly by the president and vice president

elections: president elected by popular vote for a five-year term; election last held on 17 and 24 February 2013 (next to be held in February 2018)

election results: Nicos ANASTASIADES elected president; percent of vote (first round) - Nicos ANASTASIADES 45.46%, Stavros MALAS 26.91%, Giorgos LILLIKAS 24.93%, other 2.7%; (second round) Nicos ANASTASIADES 57.48%, Savros MALAS 42.52%

note: Dervis EROGLU became "president" of the "TRNC" on 23 April 2010 after "presidential" elections on 18 April 2010; results - Dervis EROGLU 50.4%, Mehmet Ali TALAT 42.9%; Irsen KUCUK is "TRNC acting prime minister"

Legislative branch:

unicameral - area under government control: House of Representatives or Vouli Antiprosopon (80 seats; 56 assigned to the Greek Cypriots, 24 to Turkish Cypriots; note - only those assigned to Greek Cypriots are filled;

members are elected by popular vote to serve five-year terms); area administered by Turkish Cypriots: Assembly of the Republic or Cumhuriyet Meclisi (50 seats; members elected by popular vote to serve five-year terms)

elections: area under government control: last held on 22 May 2011 (next to be held in May 2016); area administered by Turkish Cypriots: last held on 19 April 2009 (next to be held in 2014)

election results: area under government control: House of Representatives - percent of vote by party - DISY 34.3%, AKEL 32.7%, DIKO 15.8%, EDEK 8.9%, EURO.KO 3.9%, other 4.5%; seats by party - DISY 20, AKEL 19, DIKO 9, EDEK 5, EURO.KO 2, other 1; area administered by Turkish Cypriots: Assembly of the Republic - percent of vote by party - UBP 44.1%, CTP 29.3%, DP 10.6%, other 16%; seats by party - UBP 26, CTP 15, DP 5, other 4

Judicial branch:

Supreme Court (judges are appointed jointly by the president and vice president); subordinate courts

note: there is also a "Supreme Court" in the area administered by Turkish Cypriots

Political parties and leaders:

area under government control: Democratic Party or DIKO [Marios KAROYIAN]; Democratic Rally or DISY [Nikos ANASTASIADES]; European Party or EURO.KO

[Demetris SYLLOURIS]; Fighting Democratic Movement or ADIK [Dinos MIKHAILIDES]; Green Party of Cyprus [George PERDIKIS]; Movement for Social Democrats or EDEK [Yiannakis OMIROU]; Progressive Party of the Working People or AKEL (Communist Party) [Andros KYPRIANOU]; United Democrats or EDI [Praxoula ANTONIADOU]

area administered by Turkish Cypriots: Communal Democracy Party or TDP [Mehmet CAKICI]; Cyprus Socialist Party or KSP [Yusuf ALKIM]; Democratic Party or DP [Serdar DENKTAS]; Freedom and Reform Party or ORP [Turgay AVCI]; National Unity Party or UBP [Irsen KUCUK]; Nationalist Justice Party or MAP [Ata TEPE]; New Cyprus Party or YKP [Murat KANATLI]; Politics for the People Party or HIS [Ahmet YONLUER]; Republican Turkish Party or CTP [Ferdi Sabit SOYER]; United Cyprus Party or BKP [Izzet IZCAN]

Political pressure groups and leaders:

Confederation of Cypriot Workers or SEK (pro-West); Confederation of Revolutionary Labor Unions or Dev-Is; Federation of Turkish Cypriot Labor Unions or Turk-Sen; Pan-Cyprian Labor Federation or PEO (Communist controlled)

International organization participation:

Australia Group, C, CD, CE, EBRD, ECB, EIB, EMU, EU, FAO, IAEA, IBRD, ICAO, ICC (national committees), IDA, IFAD, IFC, IFRCS (observer), IHO, ILO, IMF, IMO, IMSO, Interpol, IOC, IOM, IPU, ISO, ITSO, ITU, ITUC (NGOs), MIGA, NAM, NSG, OAS (observer), OIF, OPCW, OSCE, PCA, UN, UNCTAD, UNESCO, UNHCR, UNIDO, UNIFIL, UNWTO, UPU, WCO, WFTU (NGOs), WHO, WIPO, WMO, WTO

Diplomatic representation in the US:

chief of mission: Ambassador (vacant); Charge d'Affaires Olympia NEOCLEOUS

chancery: 2211 R Street NW, Washington, DC 20008

telephone: [1] (202) 462-5772, 462-0873

FAX: [1] (202) 483-6710

consulate(s) general: New York

note: representative of the Turkish Cypriot community in the US is Ahmet ERDENGIZ; office at 1667 K Street NW, Washington, DC; telephone [1] (202) 887-6198

Diplomatic representation from the US:

chief of mission: Ambassador John M. KOENIG

embassy: corner of Metochiou and Ploutarchou Streets, 2407 Engomi, Nicosia

mailing address: P. O. Box 24536, 1385 Nicosia

telephone: [357] (22) 393939

FAX: [357] (22) 780944

Key Leaders

Pres.	Nikos ANASTASIADIS

Min. of Agriculture, Natural Resources, & Environment	Nikos KOUGIALIS
Min. of Commerce, Industry, & Tourism	Georgios LAKKOTRYPIS
Min. of Communications & Works	Tasos MITSOPOULOS
Min. of Defense	Fotis FOTIOU
Min. of Education & Culture	Kyriakos KENEVEZOS
Min. of Finance	Michalis SARRIS
Min. of Foreign Affairs	Ioannis KASOULIDIS
Min. of Health	Petros PETRIDIS
Min. of Interior	Sokratis CHASIKOS
Min. of Justice & Public Order	Ionas NIKOLAOU
Min. of Labor & Social Insurance	Charis GEORGIADIS
Governor, Central Bank	Panikos DIMITRIADIS
Ambassador to the US	

Permanent Representative to the UN, New York	Nikolaos EMILIOU

Flag description:

white with a copper-colored silhouette of the island (the name Cyprus is derived from the Greek word for copper) above two green crossed olive branches in the center of the flag; the branches symbolize the hope for peace and reconciliation between the Greek and Turkish communities

note: the "Turkish Republic of Northern Cyprus" flag retains the white field of the Cyprus national flag but displays narrow horizontal red stripes positioned a small distance from the top and bottom edges between which are centered a red crescent and a red five-pointed star; the banner is modeled after the Turkish national flag but with the colors reversed

National symbol(s):

Cypriot mouflon (wild sheep); white dove

National anthem:

name: "Ymnos eis tin Eleftherian" (Hymn to Liberty)
lyrics/music: Dionysios SOLOMOS/Nikolaos MANTZAROS

<u>note</u>: adopted 1960; Cyprus adopted the Greek national anthem as its own; the Turkish community in Cyprus uses the anthem of Turkey

Chapter 5: Economy

Economy - overview:

The area of the Republic of Cyprus under government control has a market economy dominated by the service sector, which accounts for four-fifths of GDP. Tourism, financial services, and real estate are the most important sectors. Erratic growth rates over the past decade reflect the economy's reliance on tourism, the profitability of which can fluctuate with political instability in the region and economic conditions in Western Europe. Nevertheless, the economy in the area under government control has grown at a rate well above the EU average since 2000. Cyprus joined the European Exchange Rate Mechanism (ERM2) in May 2005 and adopted the euro as its national currency on 1 January 2008. An aggressive austerity program in the preceding years, aimed at paving the way for the euro, helped turn a soaring fiscal deficit (6.3% in 2003) into a surplus of 1.2% in 2008, and reduced inflation to 4.7%. This prosperity came under pressure in 2009, as construction and tourism slowed in the face of reduced foreign demand triggered by the ongoing global financial crisis. Although Cyprus lagged behind its EU peers in showing signs of stress from the global crisis, the economy tipped into recession in 2009, contracting by 1.7%, and has been slow to bounce back since, posting anemic growth in

2010-11 before contracting again by 2.3% in 2012. Serious problems surfaced in the Cypriot financial sector in early 2011 as the Greek fiscal crisis and euro zone debt crisis deepened. Cyprus's borrowing costs have risen steadily because of its exposure to Greek debt. Two of Cyprus's biggest banks are among the largest holders of Greek bonds in Europe and have a substantial presence in Greece through bank branches and subsidiaries. Cyprus experienced numerous downgrades of its credit rating in 2012 and has been cut off from international money markets. The Cypriot economy contracted in 2012 following the writedown of Greek bonds. A liquidity squeeze is choking the financial sector and the real economy as many global investors are uncertain the Cypriot economy can weather the EU crisis. The budget deficit rose to 7.4% of GDP in 2011, a violation of the EU's budget deficit criteria - no more than 3% of GDP. In response to the country's deteriorating finances and serious risk of contagion from the Greek debt crisis, Nicosia implemented measures to cut the cost of the state payroll, curb tax evasion, and revamp social benefits, and trimmed the deficit to 4.2% of GDP in 2012. In July, Nicosia became the fifth euro zone government to request an economic bailout program from the European Commission, the European Central Bank, and the International Monetary Fund - known collectively as the

"Troika". Negotiations over the final details of the plan are ongoing.

GDP (purchasing power parity):

$23.57 billion (2012 est.)

country comparison to the world: 125

$24.11 billion (2011 est.)

$23.99 billion (2010 est.)

note: data are in 2012 US dollars

GDP (official exchange rate):

$22.45 billion (2012 est.)

GDP - real growth rate:

-2.3% (2012 est.)

country comparison to the world: 206

0.5% (2011 est.)

1.1% (2010 est.)

GDP - per capita (PPP):

$26,900 (2012 est.)

country comparison to the world: 51

$28,000 (2011 est.)

$28,600 (2010 est.)

note: data are in 2012 US dollars

GDP - composition by sector:

agriculture: 2.4%

industry: 16.7%

services: 80.9% (2012 est.)

Labor force:

416,900 (2012 est.)

country comparison to the world: 159

Labor force - by occupation:

agriculture: 8.5%

industry: 20.5%

services: 71% (2006 est.)

Unemployment rate:

8% (2012 est.)

country comparison to the world: 93

7.9% (2011 est.)

Distribution of family income - Gini index:

29 (2005)

country comparison to the world: 118

Investment (gross fixed):

16.8% of GDP (2012 est.)

country comparison to the world: 126

Budget:

revenues:: $9.645 billion

expenditures:: $10.59 billion (2012 est.)

Taxes and other revenues:

43% of GDP (2012 est.)

country comparison to the world: 39

Budget surplus (+) or deficit (-):

-4.2% of GDP (2012 est.)

country comparison to the world: 135

Public debt:

80.9% of GDP (2012 est.)

country comparison to the world: 26

71.6% of GDP (2011 est.)

note: data cover general government debt, and includes debt instruments issued (or owned) by government entities other than the treasury; the data include treasury debt held by foreign entities; the data exclude debt issued by subnational entities, as well as intra-governmental debt; intra-governmental debt consists of treasury borrowings from surpluses in the social funds, such as for retirement, medical care, and unemployment

Inflation rate (consumer prices):

3.4% (2012 est.)

country comparison to the world: 95

3.3% (2011 est.)

Central bank discount rate:

1.5% (31 December 2012)

country comparison to the world: 114

1.75% (31 December 2010)

note: this is the European Central Bank's rate on the marginal lending facility, which offers overnight credit to banks in the euro area

Commercial bank prime lending rate:

7.2% (31 December 2012 est.)

country comparison to the world: 131

6.8% (31 December 2011 est.)

Stock of narrow money:

$14.73 billion (31 December 2011 est.)

country comparison to the world: 67

$14.6 billion (31 December 2010 est.)

note: see entry for the European Union for money supply in the euro area; the European Central Bank (ECB) controls monetary policy for the 17 members of the EMU; individual members of the EMU do not control the quantity of money circulating within their own borders

Stock of broad money:

$56.25 billion (31 December 2011 est.)

country comparison to the world: 66

$52.97 billion (31 December 2010 est.)

Stock of domestic credit:

$51.19 billion (31 December 2012 est.)

country comparison to the world: 64

$53.1 billion (31 December 2011 est.)

Market value of publicly traded shares:

$2.853 billion (31 December 2011)

country comparison to the world: 77

$6.834 billion (31 December 2010)

$4.993 billion (31 December 2009)

Agriculture - products:

citrus, vegetables, barley, grapes, olives, vegetables; poultry, pork, lamb; dairy, cheese

Industries:

tourism, food and beverage processing, cement and gypsum production, ship repair and refurbishment, textiles, light chemicals, metal products, wood, paper, stone and clay products

Industrial production growth rate:

0.7% (2011 est.)

country comparison to the world: 143

Current account balance:

-$1.963 billion (2012 est.)

country comparison to the world: 136

-$2.546 billion (2011 est.)

Exports:

$1.889 billion (2012 est.)

country comparison to the world: 144

$1.957 billion (2011 est.)

Exports - commodities:

citrus, potatoes, pharmaceuticals, cement, clothing

Exports - partners:

Greece 27.4%, UK 10.2%, Germany 5.5% (2011)

Imports:

$7.716 billion (2012 est.)

country comparison to the world: 108

$8 billion (2011 est.)

Imports - commodities:

consumer goods, petroleum and lubricants, machinery, transport equipment

Imports - partners:

Greece 21.7%, Israel 10.4%, UK 9%, Italy 8.3%, Germany 8.3%, France 5.7%, China 4.8%, Netherlands 4.6% (2011)

Reserves of foreign exchange and gold:

$1.207 billion (2011 est.)

country comparison to the world: 129

$1.207 billion (31 December 2011 est.)

Debt - external:

$106.5 billion (31 December 2011 est.)

country comparison to the world: 43

$113.6 billion (31 December 2010 est.)

Stock of direct foreign investment - at home:

$29.38 billion (31 December 2012 est.)

country comparison to the world: 60

$27.18 billion (31 December 2011 est.)

Stock of direct foreign investment - abroad:

$13.62 billion (31 December 2012 est.)

country comparison to the world: 50

$12.62 billion (31 December 2011 est.)

Exchange rates:

euros (EUR) per US dollar -

0.7838 (2012 est.)

0.7185 (2011 est.)

0.755 (2010 est.)

0.7198 (2009 est.)

0.6827 (2008 est.)

Fiscal year:

calendar year

Economy of the area administered by Turkish Cypriots:

Economy - overview:

The Turkish Cypriot economy has roughly half the per capita GDP of the south, and economic growth tends to be volatile, given the north's relative isolation, bloated public sector, reliance on the Turkish lira, and small market size. The Turkish Cypriots are heavily dependent on transfers from the Turkish Government. Ankara directly finances about one-third of the Turkish Cypriot "administration's" budget. Aid from Turkey has exceeded $400 million annually in recent years. The Turkish Cypriot economy experienced a sharp slowdown in 2008-09 due to the global financial crisis and to its reliance on British and Turkish tourism, both of which declined due to the recession. The Turkish Cypriot budget deficit also deteriorated in 2009 due to decreased state revenues and increased government expenditures on public sector salaries and social services. The Turkish Cypriot economy declined about 0.6% in 2010.

GDP (purchasing power parity):

$1.829 billion (2007 est.)

GDP - real growth rate:

-0.6% (2010 est.)

GDP - per capita:

$11,700 (2007 est.)

GDP - composition by sector:

agriculture: 8.6%

industry: 22.5%

services: 69.1%

(2006 est.)

Labor force:

95,030 (2007 est.)

Labor force - by occupation:

agriculture: 14.5

industry: 29%

services: 56.5%

(2004)

Unemployment rate:

9.4% (2005 est.)

Inflation rate:

11.4% (2006)

Budget:

revenues: $2.5 billion

expenditures: $2.5 billion (2006)

Agriculture - products:

citrus fruit, dairy, potatoes, grapes, olives, poultry,

lamb

Industries:

foodstuffs, textiles, clothing, ship repair, clay, gypsum, copper, furniture

Industrial production growth rate:

-0.3% (2007 est.)

Electricity production:

998.9 million kWh (2005)

Electricity consumption:

797.9 million kWh (2005)

Exports:

$68.1 million, f.o.b. (2007 est.)

Export - commodities:

citrus, dairy, potatoes, textiles

Export - partners:

Turkey 40%; direct trade between the area administered by Turkish Cypriots and the area under government control remains limited

Imports:

$1.2 billion, f.o.b. (2007 est.)

Import - commodities:

vehicles, fuel, cigarettes, food, minerals, chemicals, machinery

Import - partners:

Turkey 60%; direct trade between the area administered by Turkish Cypriots and the area under government control remains limited

Currency (code)

Turkish new lira (YTL)

Exchange rates:

Turkish new lira per US dollar: 1.668 (2011)
1.5026 (2010) 1.55 (2009) 1.3179 (2008) 1.319
(2007)

Chapter 6: Energy

Electricity - production:

4.887 billion kWh (2009 est.)

country comparison to the world: 119

Electricity - consumption:

4.698 billion kWh (2009 est.)

country comparison to the world: 117

Electricity - exports:

0 kWh (2010 est.)

country comparison to the world: 186

Electricity - imports:

0 kWh (2010 est.)

country comparison to the world: 178

Electricity - installed generating capacity:

1.392 million kW (2009 est.)

country comparison to the world: 116

Electricity - from fossil fuels:

99.7% of total installed capacity (2009 est.)

country comparison to the world: 56

Electricity - from nuclear fuels:

0% of total installed capacity (2009 est.)

country comparison to the world: 75

Electricity - from hydroelectric plants:

0% of total installed capacity (2009 est.)

country comparison to the world: 167

Electricity - from other renewable sources:

0.3% of total installed capacity (2009 est.)

country comparison to the world: 85

Crude oil - production:

0 bbl/day (2011 est.)

country comparison to the world: 125

Crude oil - exports:

0 bbl/day (2009 est.)

country comparison to the world: 102

Crude oil - imports:

0 bbl/day (2009 est.)

country comparison to the world: 176

Crude oil - proved reserves:

0 bbl (1 January 2012 est.)

country comparison to the world: 123

Refined petroleum products - production:

0 bbl/day (2008 est.)

country comparison to the world: 139

Refined petroleum products - consumption:

58,430 bbl/day (2011 est.)

country comparison to the world: 96

Refined petroleum products - exports:

0 bbl/day (2008 est.)

country comparison to the world: 171

Refined petroleum products - imports:

60,310 bbl/day (2008 est.)

country comparison to the world: 63

Natural gas - production:

0 cu m (2010 est.)

country comparison to the world: 120

Natural gas - consumption:

0 cu m (2010 est.)

country comparison to the world: 137

Natural gas - exports:

0 cu m (2010 est.)

country comparison to the world: 185

Natural gas - imports:

0 cu m (2010 est.)

country comparison to the world: 185

Natural gas - proved reserves:

0 cu m (1 January 2012 est.)

country comparison to the world: 129

Carbon dioxide emissions from consumption of energy:

9.257 million Mt (2010 est.)

country comparison to the world: 102

Chapter 7: Communications

Telephones - main lines in use:

405,000 (2011)

country comparison to the world: 105

Telephones - mobile cellular:

1.09 million (2011)

country comparison to the world: 154

Telephone system:

general assessment: excellent in both area under government control and area administered by Turkish Cypriots

domestic: open-wire, fiber-optic cable, and microwave radio relay

international: country code - 357 (area administered by Turkish Cypriots uses the country code of Turkey - 90); a number of submarine cables, including the SEA-ME-WE-3, combine to provide connectivity to Western Europe, the Middle East, and Asia; tropospheric scatter; satellite earth stations - 8 (3 Intelsat - 1 Atlantic Ocean and 2 Indian Ocean, 2 Eutelsat, 2 Intersputnik, and 1 Arabsat)

Broadcast media:

mixture of state and privately-run TV and radio services; the public broadcaster operates 2 TV channels and 4 radio stations; 6 private TV broadcasters, satellite and cable TV services including telecasts from Greece and Turkey, and a number of private radio stations are available; in areas administered by Turkish Cypriots, there are 2 public TV stations, 4 public radio stations, and privately-owned TV and radio broadcast stations (2007)

Internet country code:

.cy

Internet hosts:

252,013 (2012)

country comparison to the world: 67

Internet users:

433,900 (2009)

country comparison to the world: 120

Chapter 8: Transportation

Airports:

> 15 (2012)

> country comparison to the world: 146

Airports - with paved runways:

> total: 13

> 2,438 to 3,047 m: 6

> 1,524 to 2,437 m: 3

> 914 to 1,523 m: 3

> under 914 m: 1 (2012)

Airports - with unpaved runways:

> total: 2

> under 914 m: 2 (2012)

Heliports:

> 9 (2012)

Pipelines:

> oil 0 km

Roadways:

> total: 14,671 km

> country comparison to the world: 122

> 12,321 km under government control (includes 257 km of expressways),

> 2,350 km administered by Turkish Cypriots (2008)

Merchant marine:

> total: 838

country comparison to the world: 13

by type: bulk carrier 278, cargo 163, chemical tanker 77, container 201, liquefied gas 11, passenger 3, passenger/cargo 25, petroleum tanker 62, refrigerated cargo 5, roll on/roll off 9, vehicle carrier 4

foreign-owned: 622 (Angola 1, Austria 1, Belgium 3, Bermuda 1, Canada 2, China 6, Denmark 6, Estonia 6, France 16, Germany 192, Greece 201, Hong Kong 2, India 4, Iran 10, Ireland 3, Italy 6, Japan 16, Netherlands 23, Norway 14, Philippines 1, Poland 24, Portugal 2, Russia 46, Singapore 1, Slovenia 5, Spain 6, Sweden 5, Turkey 1, UAE 3, UK 7, Ukraine 3, US 5)

registered in other countries: 152 (Bahamas 23, Cambodia 4, Comoros 2, Finland 1, Gibraltar 1, Greece 3, Hong Kong 3, Liberia 9, Malta 32, Marshall Islands 40, Norway 1, Panama 5, Russia 13, Saint Vincent and the Grenadines 3, Sierra Leone 2, Singapore 6, unknown 4) (2010)

Ports and terminals:

area under government control: Larnaca, Limassol, Vasilikos; area administered by Turkish Cypriots: Famagusta, Kyrenia

Chapter 9: Military

Military branches:

Republic of Cyprus: Greek Cypriot National Guard (Ethniki Forea, EF; includes naval and air elements); Northern Cyprus: Turkish Cypriot Security Force (GKK) (2009)

Military service age and obligation:

Greek Cypriot National Guard (GCNG): 18-50 years of age for compulsory military service for all Greek Cypriot males; 17 years of age for voluntary service; women may volunteer for a 3-year term; length of service is 25 months (2009)

Manpower available for military service:

Greek Cypriot National Guard (GCNG):

males age 16-49: 327,875

females age 16-49: 287,891 (2010 est.)

Manpower fit for military service:

Greek Cypriot National Guard (GCNG):

males age 16-49: 275,842

females age 16-49: 239,862 (2010 est.)

Manpower reaching militarily significant age annually:

male: 8,167

female: 7,398 (2010 est.)

Military expenditures:

3.8% of GDP (2005 est.) (U)

<u>country comparison to the world</u>: 27

Chapter 10: Transnational Issues

Disputes - international:

> hostilities in 1974 divided the island into two de facto autonomous entities, the internationally recognized Cypriot Government and a Turkish-Cypriot community (north Cyprus); the 1,000-strong UN Peacekeeping Force in Cyprus (UNFICYP) has served in Cyprus since 1964 and maintains the buffer zone between north and south; on 1 May 2004, Cyprus entered the European Union still divided, with the EU's body of legislation and standards (acquis communitaire) suspended in the north; Turkey protests Cypriot Government creating hydrocarbon blocks and maritime boundary with Lebanon in March 2007

Refugees and internally displaced persons:

> IDPs: 210,000 (both Turkish and Greek Cypriots; many displaced since 1974) (2010)

Illicit drugs:

> minor transit point for heroin and hashish via air routes and container traffic to Europe, especially from Lebanon and Turkey; some cocaine transits as well; despite a strengthening of anti-money-laundering legislation, remains vulnerable to money laundering; reporting of suspicious transactions in offshore sector remains weak (2008)

. Other Key Facts™ Titles

Key Facts on Syria

Key Facts on China

Key Facts on Qatar

Key Facts on India

Key Facts on Germany

Key Facts on Argentina

Key Facts on Russia

Key Facts on North Korea

Key Facts on Brazil

Key Facts on Italy

Key Facts on the United Arab Emirates

Key Facts on the European Union

Key Facts on Pakistan

Key Facts on Saudi Arabia

Key Facts on Cyprus

Key Facts on Iran

Key Facts on Afghanistan

Key Facts on Iraq

Key Facts on Indonesia

Key Facts on South Korea

All Key Facts™ Titles are

Available at www.Amazon.com

THE INTERNATIONALIST®

2013

www.internationalist.com

www.ingramcontent.com/pod-product-compliance
Lightning Source LLC
Chambersburg PA
CBHW071649170526
45166CB00003B/1495